MEET THE
PIRATES

Liz Miles

Gareth Stevens
PUBLISHING

Please visit our website, www.garethstevens.com. For a free color catalog of all our high-quality books, call toll free 1-800-542-2595 or fax 1-877-542-2596.

Miles, Liz.
Meet the pirates / by Liz Miles.
p. cm. — (Encounters with the past)
Includes index.
ISBN 978-1-4824-0894-2 (pbk.)
ISBN 978-1-4824-0895-9 (6-pack)
ISBN 978-1-4824-0893-5 (library binding)
1.Pirates — Juvenile literature. I. Miles, Liz. II. Title.
G535.M55 2015
910.4—d23

First Edition

Published in 2015 by
Gareth Stevens Publishing
111 East 14th Street, Suite 349
New York, NY 10003

Copyright © Arcturus Holdings Limited

Editors: Joe Harris and Nicola Barber
Design: Elaine Wilkinson
Cover design: Elaine Wilkinson

Cover pictures Shutterstock:Shutterstock: background Unholy Vault Designs, pirate Jeanne McRight, compass and map Triff.

Picture acknowledgements: Alamy: p7 top Alexander McClearn; p12 Fresh Start Images; p14 Oleksiy Maksymenko; p17 top Mary Evans Picture Library; p20 and title page Theo Fitzhugh; pp21 top and 28 Lebrecht Music and Arts Photo Library. The Bridgeman Art Library: p11 top Private Collection/ Peter Newark American Pictures. Corbis: p9 bottom Derek Bayes/Lebrecht Music & Arts; p19 bottom PoodlesRock. Getty: p24 Purestock; p26 Jay P. Morgan. iStockphoto: p8 Sisoje; p10 Evanmitsui. Shutterstock: p4 background Khunaspix, top inset Meunierd, money bag Denirofoto, coins Myotis, pistol Bragin Alexey; pp5 and 28 Galyna Andrushko; pp6-7 Ruth Peterkin; p6 Viki2win; p7 bottom and title page Dudchik; pp8-9 Maria Skaldina; p9 top Tarog; pp10-11 Antonio S; pp12-13 Meunierd; p13 top atm2003; p13 bottom Jose Gil; pp14-15 Irina Kovancova; p15 top Alexander Tihonov; p15 bottom Iakov Filimonov; pp16-17 Chantal de Bruijne; p16 Chuck Wagner; p17 bottom Kenneth Summers; pp18-19 Andreas Meyer; p18 BortN66; p19 top Daniel Gale; pp20-21 Igor Sokolov (breeze); p21 bottom pzAxe; pp22-3 Alvov; p22 and title page Artincamera; p23 top and contents Rangizzz; p23 bottom Meunierd; pp24-5 Harry H Marsh; p25 top James K. Troxell; p25 bottom Chrislofotos; pp26-7 Noel Powell; p27 top Maciej Czekajewski; p29 Alexander Tihonov. Wikimedia Commons: p11 bottom Centpacrr; p27 bottom.

Printed in the United States of America

CPSIA compliance information: Batch CS15GS: For further information contact Gareth Stevens, New York, New York at 1-800-542-2595.

Contents

Into the Past

You're at home, watching a documentary on television with your family. It's all about the pirates and privateers who attacked the Spanish treasure ships in the 1600s and 1700s. As the TV program finishes, you decide to head to the kitchen for a snack... and something very strange happens!

You push the kitchen door to open it, but it's stuck. You push again, harder this time, then suddenly you are falling forwards into darkness! You're in a cold, rocky cave, echoing with crashing ocean waves. There's an oil lamp on a boulder, and next to it lies a handwritten note on a sheet of tattered paper:

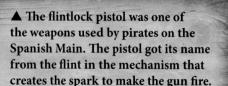

▲ The flintlock pistol was one of the weapons used by pirates on the Spanish Main. The pistol got its name from the flint in the mechanism that creates the spark to make the gun fire.

Your Mission

You're on a Caribbean island in the Spanish Main. The year is 1718CE and it is the Golden Age of Piracy. Your mission is to meet people and find out about their lives. Choose some clothes from this pile. Hurry – you only have six hours!

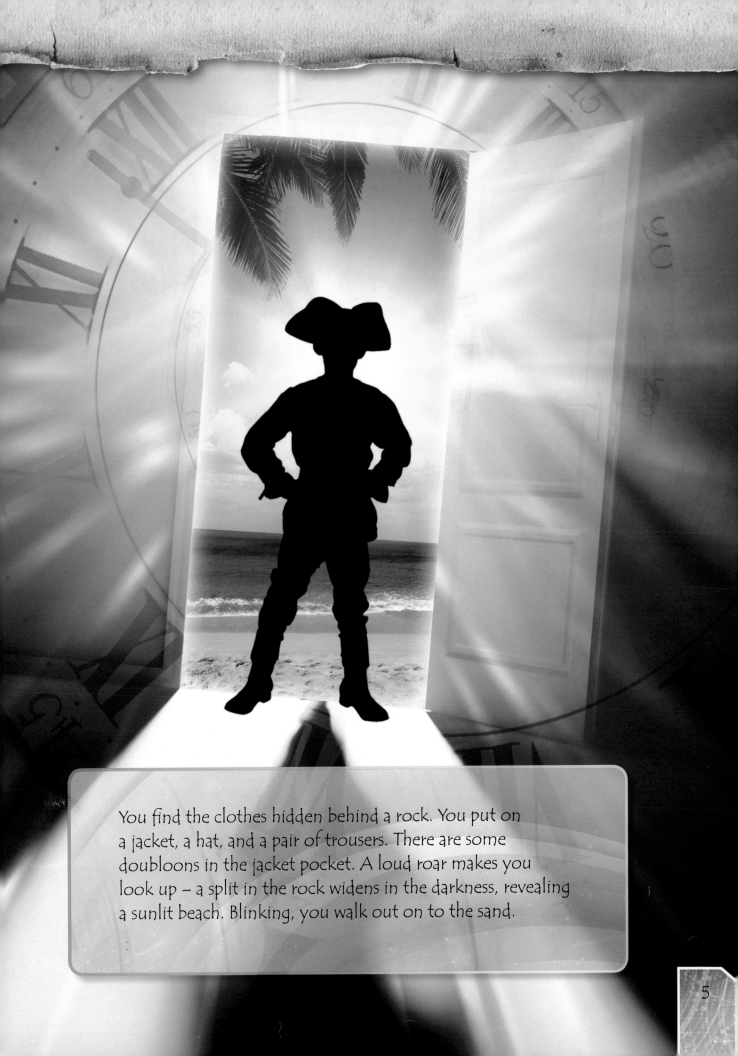

You find the clothes hidden behind a rock. You put on
a jacket, a hat, and a pair of trousers. There are some
doubloons in the jacket pocket. A loud roar makes you
look up – a split in the rock widens in the darkness, revealing
a sunlit beach. Blinking, you walk out on to the sand.

A Pirate with a Map

There's a man sitting on some rocks at the top of the beach. He beckons you over. He tells you that he is a pirate, and that his ship was wrecked during a recent skirmish with a Spanish galleon. He escaped, but with an injured leg. He can't walk far, so he asks for your help to take a map to his brother, the pirate captain of another ship. The map shows the site of the wreck – and the treasure that went down with it. You say you'll take the map if he'll answer some questions first.

WHAT WAS YOUR JOB ON THE SHIP?

I was quartermaster – that means I was next in command to the captain. I made sure the captain's orders were carried out. The crew elected me to be quartermaster, so most of the sailors respected me. Sometimes I had to break up arguments or fights, and hand out punishments. I was also in charge of sharing out the booty – making sure each pirate got a fair share of any captured goods.

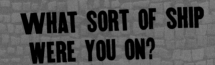

WHAT SORT OF SHIP WERE YOU ON?

The ship that was wrecked was a sloop. A sloop is a good ship for pirates because it's small, fast, and easy to steer. We hide in shallow-water bays, and take bigger, treasure-laden ships by surprise. But our sloop had only 14 cannons, while the huge Spanish galleons that attacked us had more than 60.

A sloop is small and easy to maneuver.

WHAT IS A GALLEON?

A Spanish galleon is a large sailing ship with a sturdy hull and high decks at the front and back. Galleons have three or four masts, so there is plenty of sail power, which is useful as they rely on the wind to move! They are built to carry lots of cargo, such as the treasure that makes them popular prey for pirates.

Two Spanish galleons on the high seas.

Walking with the Cabin Boy

The quartermaster calls over a boy and orders him to help you find the pirate captain. He's the cabin boy from the wrecked ship. He tells you the pirate ship is most likely moored in a port along the coast. As you set off in the direction of the port, the cabin boy warns you to be careful – if you are caught talking to pirates you may be mistaken for a pirate yourself, and punished. You ask him some questions as you walk.

WHAT'S IT LIKE TO LIVE ON A SHIP?

It's horrible most of the time. The food is bad. On long voyages, we catch and keep turtles on board for fresh meat. But by the end, there's often nothing but hardtack biscuits left – they are baked so hard it's difficult to bite them, and sometimes they have maggots inside! The bilge, which is the bottom of the ship, gets full of filthy water, and there are rats everywhere.

WHAT DO YOU DO AS CABIN BOY?

I serve the captain – fetching and carrying for him. All the time I'm learning how to be a sailor too, how to climb the rigging, how to raise and lower the sails. I know how to coil rope, and I'm teaching myself how to tie knots – I use a "cleat hitch" to secure a rope on a cleat, and a "sheet bend" to tie two rope ends together.

HOW ARE PIRATES PUNISHED?

If pirates are caught, they are often hanged in public as a warning to others and as a punishment for their crimes. I've heard that in England pirates are taken to London and hanged at Execution Dock by the River Thames. The corpses are left dangling for several days for everyone to see.

A man found guilty of piracy steps up to the scaffold at Execution Dock.

The Naval Officer

You arrive at the port. It's very busy – cargo and supplies are being loaded into several Spanish galleons. The cabin boy slips off to make inquiries about the pirate's ship. You notice a well-dressed naval officer looking out to sea through a telescope. You decide to ask him some questions.

WHAT ARE YOU LOOKING FOR?

I'm looking out for pirate ships. There are many pirates lurking in the seas and ports of our Spanish colonies in the Americas, waiting to attack our fleets. They try to steal our treasure, and they often kill our crews. I'm looking out for English ships, too, because they raid islands and settlements all along the Spanish Main.

WHERE IS THE SPANISH MAIN?

The Spanish Main is the stretch of coastline that runs around the Gulf of Mexico, the Caribbean Sea, and along the coast of South America. It's where all the gold, silver, and precious gems from our mainland colonies are brought, to be loaded onto fleets of galleons. The galleons travel in convoys of about 25 at a time for safety, to transport the treasure back to Spain.

WHAT SORT OF TREASURE DO YOU CARRY?

We carry lots of gold and silver from the mines in Peru and Mexico, which are made into Spanish coins. Silver is made into *reales* or "pieces of eight" and gold into doubloons. A single galleon can carry two million pieces of eight. We also take precious gems such as diamonds, rubies, and opals, as well as other goods such as silks, sugar, tobacco, and spices.

Silver *reales*, made in Mexico, and then transported back to Spain.

Talking to the Bosun

You leave the naval officer because you can see the cabin boy waving at you. He has found the bosun of the pirate ship. The bosun has sneaked onto land to gather provisions. When he has finished, he rows both of you to the ship, which is anchored in a nearby bay. As he rows, you ask him some questions.

WHAT IS A BOSUN?

Bosun is short for "boatswain." I look after the maintenance of the ship. I make sure the ropes, rigging, and sails are all in good order, and I organize any repairs. I've just gotten new material for a torn sail. I'm responsible for dropping and raising the anchor, too, and for making sure the decks are clean.

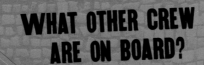

Our pirate ship is a small galleon, so we have a large crew. There are sailmakers, cooks, helmsmen who take the wheel to steer the ship, and a navigator who works out where we are going. The master gunner looks after the cannons, and boys called powder monkeys fetch and carry the gunpowder. Then there are all the able seamen – they are the sailors who go up the masts to work on the sails.

DO YOU HAVE ANY TIME OFF?

When we are at sea, there isn't much time to rest, as a ship at sail needs constant crewing. And we don't have comfortable beds to sleep in – just rough blankets on the deck. We play cards, and there might be a drop of brandy if we're lucky. A member of the crew can play the fiddle – so sometimes we all join in dancing a jig.

The Ship's Carpenter

You climb aboard the galleon and see the masts rising above you. The sails are furled because the ship is at anchor. It's busy on board, with pirates scrubbing the deck. Another pirate is counting out the crew's wages. A crowd gathers around the bosun's new provisions. But you spot someone hammering and go find out what he's doing.

WHAT ARE YOU HAMMERING?

I'm making a barrel. We use barrels to store food and drink on board. A cooper usually makes the barrels, but our cooper was lost overboard in a sea battle. I don't really have time for this! I'm the ship's only carpenter, and as the whole ship is made from wood, there's always lots of repair work.

WHAT SORT OF REPAIRS DO YOU DO?

I check the hull regularly to make sure water isn't getting in. If there is a crack, I stuff it with oakum, made from bits of old rope covered in tar, or make a wooden plug to stop the leak. I replace split planks on the decks, and make sure the masts are safe. I recently had to repair damage from a cannonball. The iron ball was fired at us from a big Spanish galleon and it made a nasty hole in the ship's side.

WHY DID YOU JOIN A PIRATE SHIP?

I make more money on a pirate ship than I can in the English navy. All of our booty is fairly divided amongst the crew. I have more power on a pirate ship, too – pirate crews often vote on matters like whether to attack a ship. And if I have a complaint, I talk to the quartermaster.

Pirate booty was shared amongst the crew.

The Sickly Rigger

The cabin boy comes over to explain that the captain is not in his cabin, so you must quickly search the ship before it sets sail. You head below deck, but soon get lost in the darkness. You jump when a face suddenly appears through a porthole in a door. A sickly-looking pirate explains that he's ill and needs blankets. You go into the cabin to help.

WHAT'S WRONG WITH YOU?

I've been ill ever since the last voyage. We had nothing to eat but dried meat and hardtack. I've got scurvy … blotches and spots all over my body and my gums are bleeding. I've heard people feel better after eating fresh food, so now the bosun has got some provisions I'll try that. I lost my eye a few weeks ago, too – I was hit by a small iron ball shot from a Spanish blunderbuss.

IS THERE A SURGEON ON BOARD?

A few pirate ships are lucky to have a surgeon, but we don't. So there's no one to help with injuries after a battle. If necessary, the carpenter cuts off injured arms or legs because he's skilled with a saw! But at least I'll get a payment for my lost eye. The crew has a fund – we pay into it so we receive money if we're injured.

The famous fictional pirate Long John Silver lost his leg during a sea battle.

WHAT WILL YOU DO?

If I eat some fresh food, I hope to feel better soon and take up my duties again. As a rigger, I need to be fit because I'm always climbing the rigging that's attached to the masts. It's my job to furl and unfurl the sails. It's a dangerous job going up and down the rigging when the ship is rolling around on a stormy sea. A fall from high up on the masts means almost certain death.

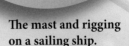

The mast and rigging on a sailing ship.

The Privateer's Story

You find some blankets for the rigger, then continue your search for the captain. You peer through the door of another cabin and a smartly dressed man beckons you in. He isn't the captain, but he is eager to tell you about his past as a privateer. He shows you a document from a locked chest as you talk.

WHAT IS A PRIVATEER?

A privateer is a kind of "legal" pirate. It's someone who has been given authority to attack ships from an enemy country. The authority comes from a government or a monarch, and is given in documents like this one, called a "letter of marque." My hero is the English privateer, Sir Francis Drake, who was licensed by Queen Elizabeth I to plunder Spanish treasure ships in the 1500s.

WHO WAS SIR FRANCIS DRAKE?

He was a sailor and explorer who became the first Englishman to sail around the world, in 1580.

He was also famous as a privateer – the Spanish called him "the Dragon." He raided ports all around the Spanish Main, and up the west coast of South America.

A statue of the explorer and privateer, Sir Francis Drake.

WHY ARE YOU A PIRATE NOW?

This letter of marque only allowed me to attack certain ships. But I decided any ship is fair game for me, not just the Spanish ships allowed by my letter. So, I became a pirate. Anyway, even if you are a privateer you still risk being found guilty of piracy! That's what happened to Captain Kidd – he was hanged as a pirate because he couldn't produce the letter of marque that proved his attacks on French ships were legal.

Captain William Kidd was found guilty of piracy, and hanged in 1701.

Pirate Disguise

You go back up on deck and run over to two friendly-looking pirates who are busy coiling ropes, and politely ask, "Excuse me sirs, do you know where the captain is?" They both roar with laughter and then whisper that they aren't "sirs" – they are women! They tell you the captain is on the poop deck, but before you rush off, you have to find out more.

WHY ARE YOU IN DISGUISE?

Women aren't allowed on ships – it's a rule. It's thought to be bad luck, and people reckon it makes the crew harder to discipline. We've both been pirates for years, on different ships. We've always dressed as men – if we wear hats, trousers, and jackets, no one knows any difference!

HOW DID YOU COME TO BE PIRATES?

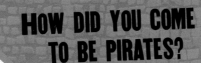

My husband was a soldier. When he died, I dressed as a pirate and found work on a pirate ship. My friend here, Anne, became a pirate when she was accused of a crime at age 13. Later, she got together with the captain of this ship, and they captured the ship I was on! So I joined the crew alongside Anne.

A female pirate in disguise.

WHAT IS LIFE LIKE FOR YOU ON BOARD?

Nobody but the captain knows that we're women. We work as hard as any man in the crew. And we're good fighters, too. In fact, we are often the only crew sober enough to fight! I'm well known for my fighting skills with a cutlass – that's this short, slightly curved sword.

Finding the Captain

You run up to the poop deck and find the captain giving orders. You hand the map over to the captain. He's very pleased to know where the wreck lies, and vows to recover the ship's treasure as soon as possible. He's in a good mood, so he's happy to answer your questions.

WHAT ORDERS WERE YOU GIVING?

I said, "All hands on deck! Weigh anchor! Look lively, you lazy bilge-suckers, or I'll have you keel-hauled!" We're off soon in pursuit of a Spanish galleon. All the crew need to be on deck to get the anchor up. A bit of name-calling and the odd threat gets them moving!

HOW DO YOU NAVIGATE THE SHIP?

We "persuaded" a sailing master from a naval ship to join us as navigator, and we use charts stolen from captured ships. These are very precious. We also have a compass and a cross-staff. The cross-staff helps the navigator to plot our position on the sea by measuring the angle between the horizon and the sun.

Some of the navigator's tools: a chart, a compass, and a telescope.

HOW DID YOU BECOME A CAPTAIN?

The previous captain was a cruel man, and eventually the crew mutinied. They marooned him by abandoning him on an island. Then they elected me to be captain – this is how we do things on pirate ships. I like to think I'm fearsome but fair. The sailors can be a wild bunch, but if they break the ship's rules, then I make sure they are punished.

Pirates were often unruly, and a pirate captain had to be tough to maintain authority over his crew.

Ship Ahoy!

Suddenly, there's a shout. The Spanish galleon has been spotted leaving port. The pirates are all busy getting ready to sail, and you must make your escape before they leave. Luckily the cabin boy is already preparing a rowing boat. While you wait, you talk to a pirate who is filling his pistol with gunpowder.

WHAT SORT OF PISTOL DO YOU HAVE?

It's a flintlock pistol. I've got five at the ready, because a flintlock needs reloading after each shot. I have a blunderbuss, too, which blasts lots of tiny metal balls in every shot.

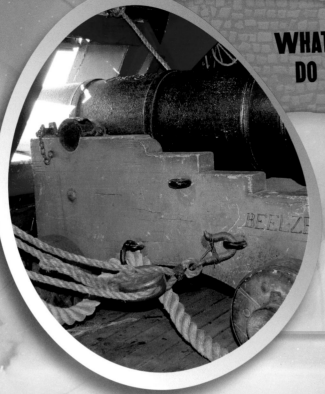

WHAT OTHER WEAPONS DO YOU HAVE ON BOARD?

We've got cannons that fire iron balls and chain-shot – that's two metal balls or half-balls joined with a chain. For hand-to-hand fighting, we have daggers, axes, and short swords called cutlasses. As we come alongside an enemy ship we throw grappling hooks, caltrops and grenadoes.

WHAT ARE GRAPPLING HOOKS?

Grappling hooks are long ropes with hooks on the end. Once the hooks are attached, we can draw the enemy ship in. Caltrops are clusters of sharp spikes. We throw them on the deck under the feet of the enemy. The sailors are usually barefoot, so the caltrops slow them down! Grenadoes are hollow iron balls filled with gunpowder. We light them and then throw them so they explode on board the enemy ship.

The Jolly Roger

You have very little time left. The sails are being unfurled and an order is given, "Up with the Jolly Roger!" A man dressed in what looks like a naval uniform with shining buttons is on lookout with a brass telescope. You quickly ask some questions while you wait for your escape on the rowing boat.

WHAT UNIFORM ARE YOU WEARING?

I used to be in the navy, but when my ship was captured by this bunch of pirates, I had little choice but to join them – or die. Now I am an able seaman on this ship. I know how to steer the ship, and all about the sails and rigging. But I'm often made to swab muck off the deck, or help repair the sails.

WHY IS THE JOLLY ROGER FLAG GOING UP?

It's to frighten the crew of the enemy ship! We would like them to surrender without a fight, so we don't risk damaging our own ship. The flag's message is: "Surrender or die!" In the past, a skull and crossbones flag was flown by ships with the deadly plague on board, to warn others to stay away.

DOES EVERY PIRATE SHIP HAVE THE JOLLY ROGER?

Pirates use all kinds of flags to terrify crews. The hourglass is a popular pirate symbol because it means "Your time is up!" Blackbeard, a fearsome pirate in these waters, has a skeleton with the devil's horns and a bleeding heart on his flag.

The pirate flag of Blackbeard, whose real name was Edward Teach.

Back to the Present

Your six hours are over. You jumped ship just as the pirates were leaving to pursue the galleon, and now you are back on the beach. You wish the cabin boy good luck, give him your doubloons, and rush into the dark cave. Inside, you quickly change back into your old clothes. Then, with a blinding flash, the door reappears and you find yourself back in the 21st century.

WERE THERE REALLY WOMEN PIRATES?

You decide to find out more about the women pirates you met on your adventure. You discover that the two most famous were Anne Bonny and Mary Read. They were captured by a British navy sloop in 1720 and put on trial for piracy. Both women escaped hanging, but there are many different accounts of what happened to them after the trial.

Anne Bonny in pirate disguise.

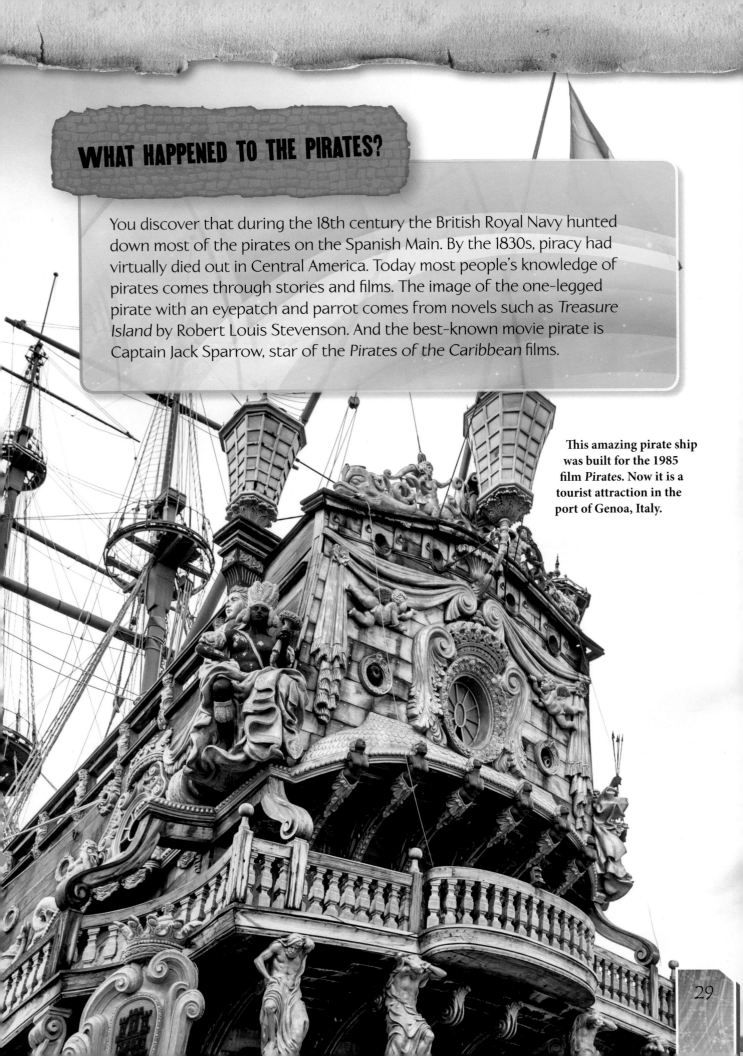

WHAT HAPPENED TO THE PIRATES?

You discover that during the 18th century the British Royal Navy hunted down most of the pirates on the Spanish Main. By the 1830s, piracy had virtually died out in Central America. Today most people's knowledge of pirates comes through stories and films. The image of the one-legged pirate with an eyepatch and parrot comes from novels such as *Treasure Island* by Robert Louis Stevenson. And the best-known movie pirate is Captain Jack Sparrow, star of the *Pirates of the Caribbean* films.

This amazing pirate ship was built for the 1985 film *Pirates*. Now it is a tourist attraction in the port of Genoa, Italy.

Glossary

able seaman An ordinary sailor in a crew who is experienced with all the routine duties on a ship.

bilge The bottom part of the inside of a ship.

blunderbuss A firearm with a long barrel which shot all kinds of ammunition such as sand, gravel, or small iron balls.

booty Goods or property seized by force or piracy.

cleat A device on a ship for securing a rope.

colony A territory under the control of a larger country.

cooper A barrel maker.

cutlass A short, slightly curved sword used by sailors.

deck An area of wood that stretches the full width of a ship, like the floor in a building.

doubloon An old gold coin, once used in Spain and South and Central America.

flintlock pistol A hand gun with a flint that caused a spark to explode the gunpowder when the trigger was pulled.

furl To roll up and secure.

galleon A large wooden sailing ship with high decks, and three or more masts. Galleons were used as cargo ships and warships.

hardtack Baked biscuits that kept for a long time, but were hard to bite.

hull The body of a ship.

keel-hauled A pirate punishment during which the victim was tied to a rope and pulled back and forth under the ship's hull, and across the keel – the lengthwise timber that supports the frame of the ship.

maroon To leave someone on an uninhabited island or coast to die.

moor To secure a boat with ropes, or an anchor, so that it can't float away.

mutiny To rebel against someone in authority by refusing to obey orders.

oakum Loose hemp or jute fiber, often obtained by untwisting old bits of rope, which is covered in tar.

plague A deadly disease that was passed to humans by the fleas that live on rats.

poop deck A raised deck at the stern (back) of a ship.

privateer A sailor who was given legal authority by a government or monarch to attack ships from enemy countries.

quartermaster In a pirate crew, the second in command to the captain.

rigging The system of ropes and chains used to support and control the masts and sails on a ship.

scurvy A disease caused by a lack of vitamin C in the diet, a vitamin found in fresh vegetables and fruit such as oranges.

sloop A small sailing boat with one mast.

Spanish Main The parts of Central America (including islands in the Caribbean Sea) and South America that were once ruled by the Spanish Empire.

swab To clean with water.

For More Information

WEBSITES

www.bonney-readkrewe.com/index.htm
Find out more about the lives of Anne Bonny and Mary Read.

www.historylearningsite.co.uk/sir_francis_drake.htm
A short biography of Francis Drake.

www.military-history.org/articles/cross-section-inside-a-16th-century-galleon.htm/
attachment/naval-gunnery-cutout
A cross-section of a 16th century English galleon.

www.nationalgeographic.com/features/97/pirates/maina.html
National Geographic: Pirates. An interactive adventure, plus information on pirate ports and Blackbeard.

www.piratesinfo.com
Pirates! Fact and Legend. A history of pirates including sections such as famous pirates.

http://pirates.hegewisch.net/
Pirates of the Caribbean. Facts and legends about pirates.

BOOKS

A 16th Century Galleon by Richard Humble (Book House, 2010)

Lives of the Pirates by Kathleen Krull (Harcourt Children's Books, 2010)

Pirate Treasure by Nick Hunt (Raintree, 2013)

Pirates Handbook by Sam Taplin (Usborne Publishing Ltd, 2014)

Sea Queens: Women Pirates Around the World by Jane Yolen
(Charlesbridge Publishing, 2010)

William Kidd and the Pirates of the Indian Ocean by John Malam (QED Publishing, 2008)

Index